The Mermaid

Written by Lisa Thompson
Pictures by Craig Smith

The mermaid dives
into the water.

The mermaid swims
in the water.

The mermaid floats
in the water.

The mermaid dances
in the water.

The mermaid jumps
out of the water.

10

The mermaid hides
behind a rock.

13

The mermaids play
hide and seek.